FODDER TO CHEW ON

BOOK TWO

BILLIE JOE

authorHOUSE®

AuthorHouse™
1663 Liberty Drive
Bloomington, IN 47403
www.authorhouse.com
Phone: 1-800-839-8640

First published by AuthorHouse   9/19/2011

ISBN: 978-1-4634-0573-1 (sc)
ISBN: 978-1-4634-0572-4 (e)

Library of Congress Control Number: 2011908277

Printed in the United States of America

Any people depicted in stock imagery provided by Thinkstock are models, and such images are being used for illustrative purposes only. Certain stock imagery © Thinkstock.

This book is printed on acid-free paper.

All quoted Scripture is from the Authorized King James version of the Bible unless otherwise noted. Quotations from The Living Bible are identified by: TLB.

CONTENTS

SAVED BY GRACE – JUDGED BY WORKS

"It is appointed unto men once to die, but after this the judgment" and "judgment must begin at the house of God." (Hebrews 9:27, 1 Peter 4:17)

Judgment usually is thought of as God's punishment of mankind for rebelling against Him. Even so, God gives mankind "space to repent" before pronouncing sentence. (Revelation 2:21)

Grace usually is defined as God's unmerited (undeserved) favor (a free gift) toward mankind – His love, kindness, consideration, mercy (clemency, compassion), etc., toward us – and He expects us to pass it on to others. (Luke 6:35-36, Acts 20:32, 2 Corinthians 6:1, Hebrews 4:16)

We are saved by God's grace through faith in the Lord Jesus Christ. God even gives us the faith to be saved. Salvation is a gift of God. (Romans 12:3, Ephesians 2:4-10, Titus 2:11)

Grace enables us to persevere in our Christian walk, to retain our righteousness when we have done something we should not have done. It saves us from condemnation, but we must repent when we realize what we did was wrong. (Acts 8:22, Romans 8:1)

We saved are ambassadors for Christ and labourers together with God. Our good works cannot save us, yet we are saved unto good works for faith without works is dead. (2 Corinthians 5:20, 6:1, Ephesians 2:10, James 2:26)

Each of us must give an account to God of the life we lived on earth. (Matthew 12:36-37, Romans 14:12)

When we leave here, our works – good and bad – follow us. We will be judged according to our works and reap the results. (1 Corinthians 3:8-9, Galatians 6:7-9, 1 Peter 1:17, Revelation 14:13, 20:13)

That can be a frightening prospect.

There will be separate judgments for those destined for hell and those destined for heaven.

Jesus Christ is our Judge. Father God has honored Jesus by committing all judgment to Him because of all He suffered and sacrificed on the cross to redeem mankind (to redeem us) that we might have life everlasting through Him. Christ will judge the world with righteousness and the people with equity. (Psalms 98:9, John 3:16, 5:22, Romans 2:16, 14:10)

The Great White Throne Judgment will be after the Millennium and after the devil has been cast into the lake of fire forever. This judgment will be for the resurrected dead of all the ages whose final destination is hell. Those people condemned themselves by rejecting Jesus Christ our only Savior, but they will acknowledge Him and bow to Him before they are cast into the lake of fire forever. (For information on the millennium, see my book FODDER TO CHEW ON, Book One, Chapter "It Is Not Armageddon.") (Mark 9:46, John 3:18, Acts 4:12, Revelation 20:1-15)

"For it is written, As I live, saith the Lord, every knee shall bow to me, and every tongue shall confess to God." "Wherefore God also hath highly exalted him, and given him a name which is above every name: That at the name of Jesus every knee should bow, of things in heaven, and things in earth, and things under the earth; and that every tongue should confess that Jesus Christ is Lord, to the glory of the Father." (Acts 10:42, Romans 14:11-12, Philippians 2:9-11, Revelation 20:13-15)

I've heard it said many times, God is not angry. He put everything – sin, sickness, disease, everything – on Jesus when He was sacrificed (crucified) on the cross and that appeased God, so we do not need to be concerned about God bringing judgment on the earth, including mankind. They are wrong.

God does not have to be angry to execute judgment. It is a matter of Him keeping His Word - doing what He said He would do. (Numbers 23:19)

Whatever God speaks forth out of His mouth will come to pass in its time. He does not need to repeat it and He will not change His mind on what He has spoken (declared). Jesus said we shall live "by every word that proceedeth out of the mouth of God." (Psalms 89:34, Isaiah 46:11, Matthew 4:4, John 12:49-50)

Jesus came to do the will of His Father God and Jesus finished all God had for Him to do. I believe all of us will be given the grace to finish what God has for each of us to do if we so choose. (John 4:34, 19:30, Philippians 1:6)

God set standards for mankind's behavior to protect us and He made conditions for us to receive His blessings. It is advantageous for us to comply. (Matthew 22:36-40, Romans 13:10, Galatians 5:14)

Again, those who reject Lord Jesus can look forward to spending eternity in hell with satan. Should that happen, they can blame only themselves. (John 3:18, 14:6, Romans 10:9-10)

We who believe on Lord Jesus Christ will be spared from appearing before His Great White Throne Judgment because we are destined for heaven. When we saved stand before The Judgment Seat of Christ, we will receive our rewards based on our works while on earth. (Romans 14:10, 1 Corinthians 3:8)

Jesus said, "And behold, I come quickly; and my reward is with me, to give every man according as his work shall be." Every work shall be made manifest (revealed) and tried by fire. Good works which stand the test shall be rewarded. Works which do not stand the test shall be burned up. If all works of a person who dies in the Lord are burned up, the person still shall be saved. (1 Corinthians 3:13-15, Revelation 22:12)

I believe works include not only deeds, but character traits we exhibit to others, often without being aware of it. Such are obvious when we walk in love and live our life with integrity. (Psalms 25:21, Luke 10:30-37, Galatians 5:22-26)

Jesus said what we do for the least of persons (as the world views them), we do for Him. He said to "Let your light so shine before men, that they may see your good works, and glorify your Father which is in heaven." Jesus said to give God the glory. Do not try to grab it for yourself. (Isaiah 42:8, Matthew 5:14-16, 44-48, 7:12, Mark 9:41, James 2:14, 26)

I do not know what kind of works will be burned up. Perhaps things we went ahead with on our own when we grew impatient waiting for God's timing to do what we knew He wanted us to do, with the result we ran out ahead of God and messed up. Or things we said we were doing for God when in reality we ignored the gifts/talents God gave us and His plan for us and we did what we wanted to do – we built our own kingdom instead of God's and then we expected God to bless what we did. Maybe. I do not know. (1 Corinthians 3:8, 13-15, 7:7, 1 Peter 4:11)

A Christian's appearance before The Judgment Seat of Christ may be rather surprising, especially if some works we thought were worthy are burned up and others we thought were trivial receive rewards.

When we show grace to others, it brightens their day and ours. Little acts of kindness build up the doer as well as the recipient. And when others see Jesus in us, it may inspire them to be more like Jesus. (John 13:15, 1 Peter 2:21)

All it takes is a kind word or a smile. Or letting the person in line behind us at a checkout counter with only one or two items go ahead of us when we have a basketful. Or when we go though a door and make sure it does not hit the person behind us in the face when it closes.

Again, showing grace, doing little acts of kindness to others, is the same as doing them to Jesus. (Matthew 25:31-46)

And don't forget to smile and say a simple "thank you" when someone blesses you with a little act of grace/kindness.

We all need grace from God and others and God is pleased when we pass it on. (Matthew 7:12, Luke 6:36)

God sees and knows everything and it just may be the little acts of grace we shower upon others may accumulate into big rewards for us some day when our works are judged by Jesus.

Yes, Jesus redeemed us from the curse of the law so we undeserving, redeemed sinners live under grace through faith in Jesus Christ who voluntarily sacrificed His life (flesh) on the cross for us, but we need to be careful not to abuse our privileges under grace. Grace is not a license to sin and it does not override our necessity to stand before The Judgment Seat of Christ one day. (John 6:51, 10:17-18, Romans Chapter 6, 14:10, Galatians 3:13, Hebrews 4:16, 9:27, Revelation 20:13)

Let each of us seek God for what He wants us to do for Him and be willing, obedient and diligent to do it His way and in His timing. And along the way, "let us not be weary in well doing: for in due season, we shall reap, if we faint not." (1 Chronicles 28:9, Isaiah 1:19, Matthew 7:7, Galatians 6:9, Ephesians 4:7, 5:16-17, Philippians 1:6, 1 Peter 4:11)

With God's grace, I am sure many of us can do more for God than we think we can, if we have a mind to. That includes me.

INITIALS

I write my drafts in longhand. After editing, I enter them into the computer. That is simpler for me. I can keep my open Bible closer to my draft which makes it easier to refer to them together.

I use my own brand of shorthand. For years, when referring to the Holy Spirit, I used his initials.

I was writing late one night and had written the Holy Spirit's initials when He spoke to me in a clear, soft, sweet voice and said, "Would you use J.C.?" (Jesus Christ). I said out loud – "No."

I removed the Holy Spirit's initials every place I had written them in my draft and wrote His Name instead.

I have a (bad?) habit of writing notes in many of my books. I looked through some of them and was surprised at how many times I had written the Holy Spirit's initials. I changed all of them to His Name. Now and then I still find His initials in a book. I always replace them with His Name.

Considering how long I wrote the Holy Spirit's initials, I don't know why He did not correct me sooner.

Anyway, I no longer use the Holy Spirit's initials when referring to Him.

LEGALISM VS LOVE

The law was given to Moses by God. We call the law "The Ten Commandments." (Exodus Chapter 20, 34:1, Acts 13:39)

Without the law, there is no sin because it is by the law we know what sin is. (Romans 3:20)

We need laws to help us live in harmony. The law gives rules for moral conduct and our duty toward God and man. The law is not for the righteous, but for sinners. (1 Timothy 1:9-11)

It is impossible to keep the law. If we break one law, we are guilty of breaking all of them. The law cannot save anyone. We cannot be righteous by trying to keep the law. We are the righteousness of God by faith in the Living Lord Jesus Christ. The law of the Spirit of Life in Christ has made us free from the law of sin and death. (Romans 8:2, 2 Corinthians 5:21, Galatians 2:16, James 2:10)

The Ten Commandments are called "the ministration of death" and "the strength of sin." The law includes blessings and curses. The law was until John the Baptist. The law terminated in Jesus Christ. Christ is the end of the law for righteousness to everyone who believes, has faith, in Him. Jesus both redeemed us from the curse of the law, being made a curse for us, and fulfilled the law. (Deuteronomy 28, Matthew 5:17, Luke 16:16, Romans 10:4, 1 Corinthians 15:56, 2 Corinthians 3:7, Galatians 3:13)

Jesus summed up the law with the commandment of love: "Thou shalt love the Lord thy God with all thy heart, and with all thy soul, and with all thy mind" and "Thou shalt love thy neighbor as thyself." (Matthew 22:37-39)

Jesus said on these two commandments hang all the law and the prophets. God is love and love fulfills the law. Jesus is our example for walking in love. (Matthew 22:40, John 13:15, 1 John 4:7-11)

Under legalism, people obey the law because they have to, not from the heart because they want to. Jesus spoke of people who honor Him with their lips, but whose hearts are far from Him. Jesus said outwardly such people appear righteous unto men, but inwardly they are full of hypocrisy and iniquity. Jesus called them hypocrites and vipers. (Matthew 15:8, 23:1-39, Mark 7:6-13)

We who have confessed Lord Jesus Christ as Savior have God the Holy Spirit dwelling in us. He helps us to walk in love, so we can love others as ourselves if we so choose. Treating others the way we want to be treated is a decision of our heart. It is not based on feelings. It may be hard at first, especially if we do not like the person, but God has not told us to like anyone. He did not put "like" in our heart. He put "love" in our heart. Treating someone the way we want to be treated does not mean we have to buddy with the person if we do not want to. (Romans 5:5, 1 John 4:15-16)

When we walk in love, we allow the Holy Spirit dwelling in us to guide us in walking by faith, not by sight, thus making it easier to stay in the will of God. (2 Corinthians 5:7, Galatians 3:11)

When we walk in love, we will not break any of the commandments for love works no ill will to his neighbor. We will do the right thing. (Romans 13:8-13)

When we walk in love, we will want to obey God because we are grateful for what He has done for us and because we love Him.

When the love of God fills our heart, we willingly and cheerfully do from our heart what we grudgingly tried unsuccessfully to do under the law. (1 Chronicles 28:9, Isaiah 1:19)

Rid yourself of that legalistic spirit. Ask the Holy Spirit to help you begin the love walk now. After awhile, walking in love will become automatic.

JEWS BY ADOPTION

The Jews are "an holy people unto the Lord thy God: the Lord thy God hath chosen thee to be a special people unto himself, above all people that are upon the face of the earth." (Deuteronomy 7:6)

One reason the Jews are special is God chose them to be the birth family of His Dear Son Jesus Christ our Lord.

God called a man named Abram to be the patriarch of the Jews. God made a covenant with Abram and changed his name to Abraham. God told Abraham he would be a father of many nations and in him all families of the earth shall be blessed. (Genesis 17:4-8, 22:17-18, Matthew 1:1-25, Acts 17:24-29, Romans 4:16-17, Galatians 3:26-29)

The Lord gave land to Abraham for him and his seed forever. God changed the name of Abraham's grandson from Jacob to Israel. He fathered the twelve tribes of Israel. Today, the nation of Israel occupies only a fraction of that land. (Genesis 13:14-18, 15:18, 17:1-8, 35:10-12, 22-26, Joshua 1:2-4, Matthew 1:1-2)

God also told Abraham He will bless those who bless him and curse those who curse him. This should inspire people everywhere to bless the Jews, yet they continue to be maligned, hated and persecuted. Some nations have expressed an intention to blast Israel off the map. (Genesis 12:3)

The Lord has chosen Jerusalem, a city in Israel, as His city and He has put His Name there forever. In the day when the Lord is King over all the earth, His Throne will be in Jerusalem. (1 Kings 11:36, 2 Chronicles 33:4, Jeremiah 3:17, Zechariah 14:9)

Israel will not be blasted off the map. And it will not go well with nations which come against Israel, including those which cause Israel to part their land. (Joel 3:2, 16-21, Zechariah 12:2-9, 14:12)

We should not mess with Israel. We should support Israel.

Much of what the Jews have suffered is because they disobeyed God, murmured against Him and rejected Jesus. Even so, God continues to bless the Jews in many wonderful ways and He is fiercely protective of Israel. God's ultimate plan for Israel and all His promises to Israel shall come to pass. (Numbers 14:1-45)

Initially, God sent Jesus "to the lost sheep of the house of Israel" – the Jews. Most rejected Jesus. After Jesus was resurrected, He called Paul (Saul), a Jew, to be an apostle to the gentiles (non-Jews). (Matthew 10:6, 15:24, Acts 9:15, 10:34-36, 22:3-21, Romans 11:13)

The Holy Spirit wrote the Bible through the Jews. That is another reason we owe the Jews a debt of gratitude (2 Timothy 3:16, 2 Peter 1:21, Revelation 1:1-2)

All who are saved, Jews and gentiles (non-Jews) – who believe in their heart Jesus is the Son of God, Jesus died for our sins and God raised Him from the dead, and have confessed Jesus as Savior – are Abraham's seed (spiritual children), heirs of the promises and the Kingdom of God through Jesus, and joint-heirs with Jesus according to God's covenant with Abraham. Abraham was an ancestor of Jesus Christ. Since Abraham was a Jew, Jesus was a Jew. Thus, salvation is of (through) the Jews. That may be the greatest reason for showing gratitude to the Jews and blessing them. (John 4:22, Romans 4:16, 8:14-17, 11:13, 1 Corinthians 12:13,27, Galatians 3:7, 28-29, 4:4-7, Ephesians 1:5, 3:6, Colossians 1:18)

Thus, Jews and non-Jews (gentiles), male and female, who confess Jesus Christ, are spiritual children of God by faith in Jesus Christ. We are One Family, the Body of Christ, the Church whose Head is Christ. We are Christ's and Christ is God's. (John 1:11-12, Romans 10:9-13, 1 Corinthians 3:23, 8:6, 10:17, 12:12-31, Galatians 3:26-29, Ephesians 4:4-6, Colossians 1:18, 1 John 3:1-2)

I have read several times some Jews believe if they accept Jesus Christ as their Messiah (Anointed One, Savior, Lord), they must give up being Jewish. Actually, the opposite is true.

Jews who become followers of Christ (Christians) still are Jews.

Gentiles (non-Jews) who become followers of Christ (Christians) are adopted (grafted) into the Family of God and since we are the spiritual seed (children) of Abraham, a Jew, we consequently are Jews by adoption. Because of his faith in God, Abraham is the father of faith for both Jews and gentiles. Abraham is the spiritual "father of all them that believe" in Jesus Christ. (Romans 4:1-25, 10:12, 12:5, 2 Corinthians 5:17, Galatians 3:7-8, 16-29, 4:5-7, Ephesians 1:5, 3:6,14-15, 4:4-6, Colossians 3:11)

This means all Christians, all who belong to Christ, regardless of ethnic group or national origin, spiritually are One Big Jewish Family.

GRIPE – GRIPE – GRIPE

I worked with a man who loved to gripe. He griped about everything. It seemed he looked for things to gripe about. The Bible refers to such people (men and women) as murmurers and complainers. (Jude 1:16)

This man had a lovely wife and a couple of fine children. He wanted his wife to get a job and griped because she had not. Then she got a job and he griped because her working caused them to eat dinner a little later and he missed his TV programs. He had her quit her job. (Note: You may get what you want, but you have to take all that goes with it.)

Once when an appliance repairman had been called to this man's home, the man's wife called him at work when the repairman finished the job and the man left work to go home and pay the repairman. The man's wife was at home the entire time, but he would not leave her a check to write out and pay the bill. (I don't think she was irresponsible because I don't remember him griping about that and I never saw any evidence of it.) This man also wanted the change from his wife's grocery shopping.

This man made good money. They had an expensive TV, computer and other luxuries, but he was not satisfied unless he had the latest model of everything.

Also, this man lived about a day's drive from his mother's house and he and his family visited her about twice a year for about ten days at a time. The man said it had become a chore to visit his mother because she always wanted him to fix something around the house and he wanted to relax. His mother was a widow and he was her only child. He talked about living in the house someday, so he should have had an interest in keeping it in good repair. If he had spent the first two or three days of their visit doing whatever his mother wanted him

12

to do, he still would have had several days to prop up his feet and let everyone wait on him.

"By much slothfulness the building decayeth; and through idleness of the hands the house droppeth through." (Ecclesiastes 10:18)

"And when the people complained, it displeased the Lord: and the Lord heard it; and his anger was kindled…." (Numbers 11:1)

Complaining hinders what God wants to do to take care of our need. For one thing, when we are griping, we are in a negative frame of mind and cannot receive what God is trying to do for us. Complaining also indicates we are not trusting the Lord in the matter. (James 3:10)

When there is a problem, our first thought and act should be to go to God, quote Him a Scripture supporting our need and praising Him for guiding us and taking care of the matter. Continue praising God until we have the answer and the matter is resolved. Then praise Him some more.

Jesus said, "Murmur not among yourselves." (John 6:43)

Proverbs 18:7 says, "A fool's mouth is his destruction, and his lips are the snare of his soul."

Out of the abundance of the heart, the mouth speaks. (Matthew 12:34)

And in Philippians 2:14, we read, "Do all things without murmurings and disputings."

These Scriptures give very good advice, especially since the Bible is clear: we shall have whatsoever we say. (Mark 11:23)

I doubt anyone would want what they say when they are griping to come to pass.

"…let us offer the sacrifice of praise to God continually, that is, the fruit of our lips giving thanks to his Name." (Hebrews 13:15)

Oh yes, that man's wife eventually left him.

A EULOGY

When a person's sojourn on earth is over and the person departs for an eternal home, it can be a very difficult adjustment for loved ones left behind.

People who never have confessed Jesus Christ as Savior depart to be with satan forever where they are separated from God and are tormented endlessly. (Matthew 25:41, 46, 2 Thessalonians 1:8-9, Revelation 14:11)

People who have confessed Jesus as Savior depart for greener pastures and life everlasting with Jesus. (Psalms 23:2, John 3:36, 11:25-26)

This paper speaks of those who depart for heaven to spend eternity with Jesus.

A thief being crucified alongside Jesus called out to Jesus and said, "Lord, remember me when thou comest into thy kingdom." Jesus said to him, "Verily I say unto thee, Today shalt thou be with me in paradise." (Mark 15:27, Luke 23:39-43)

The apostle Paul said, "For me to live is Christ, and to die is gain" – "to be absent from the body and to be present with the Lord." (2 Corinthians 5:8, Philippians 1:21-24)

These verses say a saved person who departs is instantly with the Lord.

God is a Spirit. We are made in God's image, so we are spirit beings or living souls - we have a spirit and a soul (mind, will, emotions) and we live in a body. (Genesis 1:26-27, 2:7, Zechariah 12:1, John 4:24, 1 Corinthians 15:45, 1 Thessalonians 5:23)

Our spirit is the real person. It is in the "midst" of our body. It is the "inward man," the "hidden man of the heart" and the "heart" of a person (not the heart organ). (Daniel 7:15, Romans 2:29, 2 Corinthians 4:16, 1 Peter 3:4)

We will not cease to exist when we "die." The real you and me never will die. Someday, our spirit will depart our body to return to God who gave it to us, our soul will go with our spirit and our body will return to dust because we will not need it any more. "The body without the spirit is dead." Only the body dies, so your real departed loved one is not in that casket, but is alive with Jesus. So, why do we mourn for someone who is with Jesus and is happy? We mourn for ourselves because we miss the person, but we should rejoice because the departed is in heaven. (Genesis 3:19, Psalms 30:11, Ecclesiastes 12:7, Matthew 5:4, Luke 10:20, John 11:25-26, Romans 14:8, 2 Corinthians 5:6,8, James 2:26)

Jesus said, "I am the resurrection, and the life: he that believeth in me, though he were dead, yet shall he live: And whosoever liveth and believeth in me shall never die." (John 11:25-26)

I hear people, even Christians, say after someone has departed the person is "now an angel." No. The departed is the same person as when on earth. Since we will know each other in heaven, our appearance in heaven will be similar to what it was on earth. (Luke 16:19-31, 24:39)

I have heard people express horror over someone who departed without being sick. They usually say something like, "He was so healthy!" So? The person just left. Being sick before departing may give an opportunity to say goodbye to loved ones, to witness to others, to put personal affairs in order and fine tune one's relationship with God, but being sick is not a requirement for departing for our eternal home. We really need to stay ready to depart at any moment.

Many believe their departed loved ones watch them from heaven. I personally do not believe they know anything about the personal lives of those left behind. It is possible they have some knowledge of spiritual happenings on earth because there is joy in heaven over a sinner who repents. (Luke 15:7, 10)

One evening in church near the end of the service, a black silhouette flashed in front of my eyes and I heard the words, "Pray for my children." I knew instantly the message was from one of my departed sisters and who needed prayer.

While it is difficult to adjust to the departure of any loved one, no adjustment is harder than when a child departs.

Any child who departs under the age of accountability goes to be with the Lord, so we need to find comfort in the fact the child is with Jesus and is happy. Also find comfort in the fact we who are left behind and are saved will be reunited with the departed in heaven some day. When the son of King David and Bathsheba departed, King David said, "I shall go to him, but he shall not return to me." Being with Jesus and our loved ones in heaven for all eternity is reason enough to repent, acknowledge Jesus Christ as Savior, and get right with God. (2 Samuel 12:23, Romans 10:9-10)

I have been to funerals where the family of the departed requested an altar call at the end of the service. That is not a bad idea.

Often, some people at a funeral never have been in church, or at least not for a long time, and may not be saved. The nature of the ceremony may cause them to think about their own mortality and eternal destination. Adding an altar call to a eulogy can produce amazing results for God.

WOMAN

God "formed man of the dust of the ground, and breathed into his nostrils the breath of life; and man became a living soul." God caused a deep sleep to fall upon the man. Then God removed one of his ribs and made a woman. She was called "Woman" because she was taken out of man. (Genesis 2:7, 21-23)

The man God created was called "Adam" (rosy, red, ruddy). Adam called the woman "Eve" because "she was the mother of all living." (Genesis 3:20)

One time Jesus was talking to some people and someone told Him His mother and brethren were there and desired to speak with Him. Jesus said to the person who had spoken to Him, "Who is my mother? and who are my brethren?" Then Jesus stretched forth His hand toward His disciples and said, "Behold my mother and my brethren. For whosoever shall do the will of my Father which is in heaven, the same is my brother, and sister, and mother." (Matthew 12:46-50)

Jesus said all who do Father's will are His spiritual family. He acknowledged Mary as His mother, but He did not speak directly to her. (1 Corinthians 12:13, Galatians 3:26-29)

Jesus attended a wedding in Cana with His mother and His disciples. His mother told Jesus there was no wine. When Jesus answered her, he called her "Woman." (John 2:1-4)

When Jesus was hanging on the cross, He saw His mother and the disciple He loved (John) standing nearby. He said to His mother, "Woman, behold thy son!" And to the disciple, He said, "Behold thy mother!" From that hour, the disciple took Mary into his own home. (John 19:25-27)

Jesus addressed His mother as "Woman" and he told the disciple John to care for Mary as he would his own mother.

BILLIE JOE

In the midst of the extreme agony Jesus was suffering on the cross, He took care of His mother.

Jesus acknowledged Mary as His mother, but I cannot find where Jesus ever called Mary "Mother" when speaking directly to her. To have done so would have made Mary the mother of God – which she was not.

THE CATALYST

There is no remission of sin without the shedding of blood. Jesus shed His Innocent Blood for the remission of our sins. (Matthew 26:28, 2 Corinthians 5:21, Hebrews 9:22)

Jesus took our infirmities and bare (bore) our sicknesses, diseases and sins in His Own Body on the cross and it is by His stripes we were (are) healed. (Matthew 8:17, 1 Peter 2:24)

Before Jesus left earth to go back to Father in heaven, He said to His disciples, "Verily, verily I say unto you, Whatsoever ye shall ask the Father in my name, he will give it you." (John 16:23)

In John 14:13-14, Jesus said, "And whatsoever ye shall ask (Father) in my name, that will I (Jesus) do, that the Father may be glorified in the Son. If ye ask any thing in my name, I (Jesus) will do it." He said something similar in John 15:16.

There is no name above the Name of Jesus. There is no other name under heaven whereby people must be saved. Jesus is "the way, the truth and the life: no man cometh unto the Father, but by" Jesus. (John 14:6, Acts 4:12, Philippians 2:9)

We are to live by faith in the Word of God. We are to walk by faith, by what the Word says, not by what we see. We are to have faith in the Name of Jesus. And when we ask Father for something, we are to ask Him in the Name of Jesus. (Acts 3:16, 2 Corinthians 5:7, Hebrews 10:38)

These Scriptures say we are to ask Father in the Name of Jesus to grant our petitions. Let's look at other Scriptures.

When Jesus sent seventy out in pairs to heal the sick, they said when they returned, "even the devils are subject unto us through thy name." (Luke 10:1-17)

In Acts 3:6, the apostle Peter said, "In the name of Jesus Christ of

Nazareth rise up and walk." He said in Acts 9:34, "Jesus Christ maketh thee whole: arise, and make thy bed. And he arose immediately."

In these Scriptures, they did not ask Father in the Name of Jesus. Instead, they commanded something be done in the Name of Jesus.

Why do we sometimes ask Father for something in the Name of Jesus and other times we command something be done in the Name of Jesus?

In Acts 1:8, Jesus told the apostles, "But ye shall receive power, after that the Holy Ghost is come upon you: and ye shall be witnesses unto me both in Jerusalem, and in all Judea, and in Samaria, and unto the uttermost part of the earth."

When the seventy mentioned above returned, Jesus told them, "Behold, I give unto you power to tread on serpents and scorpions, and over all the power of the enemy: and nothing shall by any means hurt you…rejoice not, that the spirits are subject unto you; but rather rejoice, because your names are written in heaven." This same power has been given to all who are saved (Christians). (Luke 10:19-20, Acts chapter 2)

Jesus said in Mark 16:17-18, "And these signs shall follow them that believe; In my name shall they cast out devils; they shall speak with new tongues; They shall take up serpents; and if they drink any deadly thing, it shall not hurt them; they shall lay hands on the sick, and they shall recover."

Jesus came "that he might destroy the works of the devil." He redeemed us from the curse of the law and overcame the world. He said we who believe on Him shall do greater works than He did. (John 14:12, 16:33, Galatians 3:13, 1 John 3:8)

Before Jesus went back to heaven, He delegated some of His works to all Christians – to us who are His representatives on earth and labour together with God. (Mark 16:17-18, 1 Corinthians 3:9, 2 Corinthians 5:20)

We are to do the work of Jesus in His Name and He delegated authority to us to use His Name to accomplish His work, as evidenced already. (Matthew 24:14, John 14:12)

When we (all Christians) are doing the work Jesus delegated to us and we give a command in the Name of Jesus, it is the same as Jesus Himself giving the command, so it is not necessary to ask Father beforehand. It is necessary to do the work of Jesus in the Name of Jesus. (Colossians 3:17)

On the other hand, if we want Father God to do something Jesus did not delegate to us, we are to present our request (desire, petition) to Father and ask Him to grant it in the Name of Jesus. Then we are to believe we have received it and thank Father for it in the Name of Jesus, and continue to thank Him until we get it. And even after we get it. (Mark 11:22-26, Hebrews 4:16)

The apostles did not ask Father before they commanded people to be healed in the Name of Jesus, cast out devils in His Name, etc., because Jesus already had given them authority/power to do those things in His Name.

So – it is not necessary for believers in Jesus Christ to ask Father to do things Jesus has delegated to us to do in His Name.

And if something is promised in God's Word, such as healing, we do not need to pray "if it be thy will," because God already said it is His will to heal people and to do everything else His Word says He will do. (1 Peter 2:24, 1 John 5:14-15)

We are to ask Father in the Name of Jesus to do things Jesus did not delegate to us such as to give us the ability to do whatever He calls us to do, to guide us in His plan for our life, whether we should buy a particular vehicle, marry a particular person, etc., etc.

Then listen to what God the Holy Spirit says and obey Him.

God's Word is the Will of God. If we ask anything according to His Will (Word), He hears us and if we know He hears us, whatsoever we ask, we know we have the petition we desire of Him. It is important to back up our request with Scripture and quote the Scripture to God when we make our petition. (Asking God to support our sin is not God's Will.) (Psalms 37:4-5, Isaiah 43:26, Mark 11:22-26, 1 Peter 4:11, 1 John 5:14-15)

Also, we are to praise Father God and to thank Him in the Name of Jesus for answering our prayers. We are to give thanks always for all things unto God and the Father in the Name of our Lord Jesus Christ. That includes things we command in the Name of Jesus. (Ephesians 5:20, 1 Thessalonians 5:17-18)

Colossians 3:17 says, "And whatsoever ye do in word or deed, do all in the name of the Lord Jesus, giving thanks to God and the Father by him." (Hebrews 13:15)

Whether we are asking Father God for something or praising Father, whether we are using the authority Jesus delegated to us, or whether we are confessing the Word we are standing on when believing for something we petitioned Father to give us, we are to do it in the Name of Jesus. We are to have faith in the Name of Jesus if we are to be effective in our efforts for God and successful in having our prayers answered. (Mark 11:22-26, Acts 3:16, Galatians 2:20)

Jesus Christ is the Son of God, Jesus is the Word of God. All power has been given to Jesus in heaven and in earth. That power is in His Name. We are to believe on the Name of Jesus and, again, to have faith in the Name of Jesus. (Matthew 28:18, John 1:1-18, Acts 3:16, 1 John 3:23, 5:13-15, Revelation 19:13)

So – there are times we ask Father to do something in the Name of Jesus and there are times we command something to be done in the Name of Jesus. And always, we praise God in the Name of Jesus. (Hebrews 13:15)

"Thanks be to God, which giveth us the victory through our Lord Jesus Christ." (1 Corinthians 15:57)

The catalyst, then, that gives us victory over the world is the Name of Jesus. (Revelation 12:11)

Use the Name of Jesus often, responsibly and reverently.

THE WOMAN AT THE WELL

You may recall the conversation Jesus had with the woman at the well. She had been MARRIED five times and was then living with a man not her husband. (John 4:1-43)

I have heard more than one speaker say from the pulpit the reason she had been married so many times was because her needs were so great, no one man could satisfy her. My Bible does not say that.

I also have heard it said from the pulpit the woman had slept with every man around and was a prostitute. My Bible does not say that either and I will not so label her.

My Bible does not say if any of her husbands had died. Suppose some had and some had not.

In that woman's day, so I read somewhere, a husband could divorce a wife for any trivial thing she did which displeased him.

A divorced wife was sent from her husband's house without any real means of support until she could get reestablished. She was free to remarry and I imagine many divorced women were desperate to do so for their survival. (I also read somewhere women wore all their jewelry all the time because they could be made to leave with only what they were wearing.)

Also, according to the custom of that day, if a man departed and he had no children, his brother or nearest kinsman married the departed's widow and produced children in the departed's name. That was the situation with Naomi whose husband and two sons had departed and she had no other sons for her daughters-in-law to marry. She told each daughter-in-law to return to her mother's house. One, Oprah, did, but the other, Ruth, was determined to stay with Naomi, so Ruth went with Naomi to Naomi's home. Eventually, Ruth married Naomi's kinsman Boaz and became an ancestor of Jesus. (Book of Ruth)

Another instance of this custom concerns Onan. (Genesis 38:6-26)

The Sadducees addressed this custom to Jesus citing a hypothetical woman who married seven brothers and all departed without children. Then she departed. They wanted to know whose wife she would be in heaven. (Luke 20:27-38)

I think the reason for this custom was to keep property in the family.

I do not know why this woman had been married multiple times. I do not know whether she had been divorced or widowed, or both. My Bible does not say. If she had been widowed, the established custom probably prevailed. If she had been divorced, well, I thought of one possibility.

There is no indication this woman had children. Women were expected to have children. Their value often was tied to how many children they had. If this woman was indeed divorced, it may have been for failure to have children. I do not know.

Whatever the reason(s) for this woman's multiple marriages, it seems she had given up on marriage because she was living with a man without being married to him.

When Jesus told the woman about herself, she became excited, left her water pot (her work), went into the city and testified to what Jesus had told her. She said, "Come, see a man, which told me all things that ever I did: is not this the Christ?" They went to see and many Samaritans believed on Jesus because of the woman's testimony. They asked Jesus to tarry with them and He stayed two days.

According to John 4:1-43, these are the facts about the woman at the well – without the fanciful ideas of some speakers.

JUDGE THE ACT - NOT THE DESTINATION

Jesus said, "Judge not, that ye be not judged." (Matthew 7:1)

The apostle Paul said, "every one of us shall give account of himself to God" and "if we would judge ourselves, we should not be judged." (Romans 14:12, 1 Corinthians 11:31)

So, we should not judge others, but we should judge ourselves.

We need to deal with ourselves and keep sin out of our lives. We need to be quick to repent, quick to forgive, quick to apologize and then quick to forget because God forgot our sin when we repented. We also need to be quick to obey God. (Isaiah 43:25, Philippians 3:13)

Even though we must not judge whether someone's destination will be heaven or hell, we must deal with our problems.

Jesus said if a brother (Christian) sins against you, talk to him alone about it. If that takes care of the problem, you have won back a brother, but if it does not take care of the problem, take one or two with you and talk with him again. If that does not resolve the problem, tell the church. If still no resolution, "let him be unto thee as an heathen man and a publican." (Matthew 18:15-17)

Paul also spoke about brothers (Christians) suing brothers (Christians) and unbelievers witnessing it. Paul's advice was, "Why do ye not rather take wrong? why do ye not rather suffer yourselves to be defrauded?" (1 Corinthians 6:6-7)

It is not a good witness for the Lord when Christians get into a court fight or any other fight. We must ever be mindful our witnessing for the Lord should follow the example Jesus gave us. (I think we all can improve our witnessing for the Lord. I know I can.) (John 13:15)

If a person is overtaken in a fault, we who are "spiritual" should "restore such an one in the spirit of meekness, considering thyself, lest thou also be tempted." We should try to restore someone who is doing wrong, but we must be careful not to succumb to the same fault/sin. (Galatians 6:1)

The apostle Paul told the Corinthian church it was common knowledge there was fornication among them and the church had not taken care of it. Paul said even though he was "absent in body," he was "present in spirit" and he had judged the situation as though he physically were present. He said such a person should be delivered "unto satan for the destruction of the flesh, that the spirit may be saved in the day of the Lord Jesus." Paul judged the sin and left the person's final destination open. He wanted whoever was involved to repent and get right with God. (1 Corinthians 5:1-5)

Eli was an Old Testament priest. He had two sons who did not know the Lord and did evil. Eli knew it, but he did not control them. The Lord judged Eli and his "house for ever for the iniquity which he knoweth; because his sons made themselves vile, and he restrained them not." Eli and his sons died. (1 Samuel 2:12—4:22)

We should not ignore problems when we have authority to do something about them, but it is one thing to judge an act and another thing to try to judge where a person will spend eternity. Only God knows where someone will spend eternity.

When our daughter was about five years old, the kids in the neighborhood were collecting rubber bands to make Chinese jump ropes. One day, I heard her running up the walk. She was wailing. I opened the front door and she ran past me and fell into a heap on the living room floor. Behind her was an angry, young Air Force officer. He told me she had stolen the rubber band off his newspaper. He said she would be a criminal and spend her life in prison. I thanked him for telling me, he left and I closed the door.

I told our daughter it was wrong to take a rubber band off someone's newspaper even if it was on the sidewalk. The paper could have blown all over the neighborhood. I told her she must ask the owner of the paper if she could have the rubber band.

Then I had her take the rubber band to the man's house, ring his doorbell, give the rubber band to him and apologize for taking it. I went with her and waited on the sidewalk while she went to his door. Then I took her hand and we went home. She had learned a valuable lesson and all had been forgiven (by me, anyway).

Except for telling her dad when he came home from work, I don't recall mentioning it again until I told the story to her children (in her presence).

I judged our daughter's act, but the young officer judged her future. Of course, none of what he said came true. She is a fine Christian lady.

Sometimes, we must judge what a person does, but never speculate where someone will spend eternity.

I believe when we get to heaven, we will be surprised at who is there and who is not. Some reprobates will get saved somewhere along the way and be in heaven, and some people who attend church regularly never will confess Jesus, so will be denied entry into heaven. (Matthew 7:21-23, 19:30, John 14:6)

Judging ourselves will keep us busy. Leave judging others to Jesus.

IRRESPONSIBILITY IS NOT A VIRTUE

Most of us know people who are charming, but completely irresponsible when it comes to honoring their word.

They say they will do something, but do not do it. (Psalms 63:11, Zechariah 8:16-17)

They arrive late to everything, usually without apology when they finally show up. It seems not to bother them at all to keep a host/hostess waiting, trying to keep dinner from being ruined, to say nothing of inconveniencing other guests.

I am not talking about people who arrive a few minutes late to allow the host/hostess time to complete everything if running behind schedule. Proper etiquette supports that. I'm talking about people who are always LATE.

Of course, there may be times someone cannot avoid being late due to a flat tire, etc. We are tolerant of those people because there is a valid reason. Those people will try to let us know they will be late and genuinely apologize when they arrive.

Irresponsible people borrow things and do not return them. Expensive things. Valuable things. (Psalms 37:21)

A lady from church borrowed a reference book I could not replace. She promised to return it. She did not. I called her more than once. Then I told her I would take her to lunch and she could return the book at that time. She met me for lunch, but "forgot" the book. Again, I took her to lunch and again she came without the book. She seemed determined to keep the book and I was determined to get it back. Eventually, I got it back. I'm friendly if I see her, but I do not want to buddy with her.

Irresponsible people lose things. Important things. Things which cannot be replaced. Then they make light of it – they treat it as a joke and get offended if asked about it.

29

Irresponsible people say things like, "That's just the way I am," meaning they don't care about anyone but themselves and what they want.

God's Word is infallible. God's Word is His reputation. If we cannot trust God's Word, we cannot trust God. It is the same with us and our word.

Our word is our reputation.

"He that is faithful in that which is least is faithful also in much: and he that is unjust in the least is unjust also in much." We often are tested on small things before we are trusted with greater things – tested by parents, employers, even those we might want to marry, and by God. (Luke 16:10-13, 2 Timothy 2:2)

There was a time not long ago when people sealed high-dollar contracts with a handshake. Now it takes a pack of lawyers to execute a contract.

"A fool's mouth is his destruction, and his lips are the snare of his soul." (Proverbs 18:7)

"Suffer not thy mouth to cause thy flesh to sin...." (Ecclesiastes 5:6)

People who are irresponsible with their word may be sinning without realizing it.

"Put away from thee a froward mouth, and perverse lips put far from thee." (Proverbs 4:24)

Jesus speaking: "But I say unto you, That every idle word that men shall speak, they shall give account thereof in the day of judgment. For by thy words thou shalt be justified, and by thy words thou shalt be condemned." (Matthew 12:36-37)

Irresponsibility is not a virtue. Maybe we all need to examine ourselves to discover how often we do the right thing and honor our word.

MY VERY SPECIAL FRIEND

I was asked to give a lady a ride to church. I did and that was the beginning of a very special and beautiful friendship.

I will call her "Maryanne" which is not her name.

Maryanne was born in Hawaii. When I met her, she and her husband had three grown children, a daughter and two sons.

Maryanne had polio when she was pregnant with their second child. She walked with a brace on one leg and used crutches when she went outside the house.

Maryanne is a fabulous cook and, at that time, she enjoyed making bread and oriental dishes. At Christmas, she made cookies and I made candy and we shared. Her sand tarts were my favorite.

One time when my daughter and I were going out of town for a few days, Maryanne and her husband offered to care for my daughter's goldfish. We took the fish to their house, but forgot the food. Her husband said he would take care of it. When we picked up that fish, it had almost doubled in size from the dog food he had fed it.

Maryanne decided she wanted to learn to drive. She told her husband she wanted to use their car only one or two days a week. He was not enthusiastic about it.

Maryanne could carry a small bag with a handle with her crutches, but she could not manage anything heavy such as grocery bags. In the main, she wanted a little independence. After she began driving, she enjoyed going to gift shops and shopping for cards by herself. She could take all the time she wanted to read them and not feel rushed in selecting the perfect card. But getting to that place was an ordeal.

Maryanne's husband was concerned about her driving and he put many obstacles in her way. He told her she did not know how to drive. She took driving lessons and got her license. He told her she would need hand brakes. She got hand brakes, but her husband did not have them installed. Every time Maryanne met one condition, he came up with another. After months of frustration from meeting her husband's conditions and still not having a vehicle to drive, Maryanne called me, said she was leaving and asked me to take her to the airport. She had a destination in mind – a visit with a friend she had known for years. I went to Maryanne's house, but talked her out of leaving.

Maryanne found a vehicle she wanted, but her husband was in the hospital. I don't recall his problem being life threatening. Anyway, she sent the salesman to the hospital to have her husband sign the papers to purchase the vehicle. He did.

Maryanne is an excellent driver and she really enjoyed driving that vehicle and the freedom it gave her. Later, she had a van with a lift so she could put a scooter in the back.

Often, the three of us – Maryanne, my daughter and I – would have Sunday brunch before church. The buffet choices were almost staggering in quantity and all were delicious. We still reminisce about how much we enjoyed those times.

When it was time for Maryanne's husband to retire from the Air Force, they wanted to buy a house. I saw one for sale I thought they would like and they bought it. They lived there for many years until Maryanne's husband died. Then Maryanne moved to another part of the state to be near one of their children.

Maryanne and I are as close as ever even though our contact is limited now by distance.

There are many other stories I could share, but our most memorable times are the hours we have spent talking about the Bible and the work God is doing in the earth.

In spite of many heart-rending life occurrences and limitations caused by polio, Maryanne always has a cheerful smile, a sunny disposition and a sense of humor. She never complains.

Maryanne told me she looks forward to running on the beach again one day. I believe she will – one day.

BEWARE THE DEVIL

The line, "The devil made me do it," was made famous by the comedian Flip Wilson. Every time he said it, it drew peals of laughter. The sad thing is, there is a lot of truth in that line.

There are two kinds of people in the world: those who belong to Jesus Christ and those who belong to satan (the devil).

God loves all of us unconditionally and He gives us the freedom to choose the kind of life we want to live. Some choose to live for Jesus. Others choose to live with satan.

People reject Jesus because they enjoy their life of sin and do not want to give it up. Or maybe they do not believe what they have been taught about Jesus. Regardless, every one of us eventually will have to answer to Jesus for our life lived on earth. (Romans 14:10, Hebrews 9:27)

I heard a famous actor say on television he had a reputation as a womanizer, a boozer and a hell raiser and he thought that was a good reputation to have. I wonder what he thinks now that he has gone to his eternal home.

Even those who decide to live life their way need to know what God's Word says so they can make a more enlightened choice of where they want to spend eternity. (Matthew 10:28, 16:26)

Many of us wish some Scriptures were not in the Bible, but they are and we cannot live for God and pick and choose which we will accept and obey and which we will ignore. God said what He meant to say and means what He said. (Numbers 23:19)

Satan, the devil, is real. He is our adversary. He is the deceiver of the whole world. He twists the Word of God just enough to cause doubt and "beguile" people as he did Eve. He makes people think they are missing something good if they say "no" to sin. (Genesis 3:13, 2 Corinthians 4:3-4, 11:3, 1Timothy 2:14, Revelation 12:9)

Satan harasses Christians. He cannot possess a Christian unless invited in. (The saved are the temple of the Holy Spirit and satan and the Holy Spirit cannot dwell in the same house.) Satan can hinder the work of God's people. The apostle Paul was "buffeted" by one of satan's messengers. (John 14:16-17, 1 Corinthians 6:19, 2 Corinthians 12:7, 1 Thessalonians 2:18)

Satan causes physical suffering. (Acts 10:38)

Satan and his demons talk to people. Some people in the news who were convicted of heinous crimes said they heard voices and those voices told them to commit the crimes. They may have been possessed by satan at the time they committed those crimes. Judas gave himself over to satan and betrayed Jesus. (Luke 8:26-36, 22:3-4, 47-48, John 13:1, 21-28)

Many people erroneously accept satan's voice for God's voice. One big difference is satan is a master at tricking people, but God never will trick people or compromise His Word. God never will try to get someone to do something wrong. God cautioned us to "try the spirits whether they are of God." Jesus said His sheep know His voice, but Christians still can allow themselves to be duped by satan. Never ask to hear voices and be very cautious if you do hear voices. Verify what you hear with God's Word and disregard everything which does not agree with God's Word. (John 10:1-5, 1 John 4:1-4)

Satan has blinded eyes and hardened hearts to the truth of God's Word and caused people to believe wrong is right and not to take God's Word seriously. As a result, many living in sin think they are living righteously. (Proverbs 16:25, Matthew 7:13-14, John 12:40, Acts 26:18, 2 Corinthians 4:4)

When God finished creating the heavens and the earth, He beheld everything He had made and it was "very good." God loves all people unconditionally, but He hates evil. When people choose to turn from God, they become separated from Him and get into evil conduct

God cannot accept because it is abominable to Him. (Genesis 1:31, 2:1, Proverbs 8:13, Amos 5:14-15)

God is patient with sinners and He gives them space to repent. If people do repent and turn from their sinful ways, God will forgive them, accept them into His Family and forget all about their past. God will forgive any and all sin regardless of how heinous. He will not turn away any person who repents. (Isaiah 43:25, Jonah 3:10, Matthew 7:13-14, John 6:37, 1 Corinthians 6:11, 2 Corinthians 5:17, 2 Thessalonians 1:6-10, 2 Peter 3:9, Revelation 2:21)

If people will not repent, if they continue to refuse the Holy Spirit's efforts to get them to repent, God eventually will turn them over to their reprobate mind and let them go their own way which leads to destruction. For those people, their long-term future is dark and relentlessly agonizing. (Matthew 7:13, Romans 1:15-32)

"The wrath of God is revealed from heaven against all ungodliness and unrighteousness of men, who hold the truth in unrighteousness." (Romans 1:18)

God said if backbiters, the unbelieving, the fearful, liars, whoremongers and many others, including men and women whose lust causes them to dishonor their bodies in ways which are against nature, do not repent, they and others "shall have their part in the lake which burneth with fire and brimstone" (hell). Since this is only a partial list, I suggest you read these Scriptures: Leviticus 18:22-23, 19:28, 20:13, Deuteronomy 18:9-12, Matthew 10:32-33, 18:3, Luke 17:26-30, Romans 1:24-32, 1 Corinthians 6:9-11, Galatians 5:19-21, Colossians 3:5-10, 25, 2 Thessalonians 1:8-9, 1 Timothy 1:8-10, 2 Timothy 3:1-17, Revelation 21:7-8.

"And such (of the above) were some of you," but you repented and Jesus Christ delivered you by His sacrifice on the cross and by your acceptance and confession of Him as your Savior. You became a new creature in Christ with your entire past remitted (erased) and all things made new! God and God only can forgive our sins and deliver us from everything we need deliverance from and He will if we just repent and ask Him. That includes ALL the wrong things we have done and the aftereffects of things done to us, even sexual abuse and post-traumatic stress syndrome. It really is as simple as it sounds. (Matthew 18:3, 1 Corinthians 6:11, 2 Corinthians 5:17, 1 John 3:8)

Let me repeat: Ask God to forgive you of all the wrong you have done and deliver you from all your bad habits and the aftereffects of what others have done to you. Then go on with God, be the person God wants you to be and don't look back. Ask Him to start you on the work He has for you to do for Him and to give you the ability to do it. (Galatians 2:20, Philippians 3:13-14, 1 Peter 4:11, 1 John 4:4)

Don't carry around guilt and shame over things God has forgiven and delivered you from when God has forgotten all about them. Whatever God has forgotten, you forget. (Isaiah 43:25)

When Jesus Christ the Precious Son of God sets you free, you are free indeed. Not free to sin, but free to live for God. Free to live peacefully and joyfully in the Lord. (Psalms 35:9, Isaiah 61:10, John 8:36, Romans 8:2, 14:17, Galatians 5:1)

Every time satan brings to your mind something God has forgiven or delivered you from, thank satan for reminding you how great God is for setting you free from the bondage you were in. Then thank God for setting you free. After a few times, satan will back off, at least for a while. (Luke 4:13)

Satan is no joke. He is real. And he is intent on devouring us and taking us to hell with him, but Jesus has given us power over the devil. When we submit to God and resist the devil, he will flee. Exercise your authority over the devil. (John 8:44, 10:10, James 4:7, 1 Peter 5:8-9)

I believe we are nearing the end of this Church Age and the closer we get to the end, the greater the increase in the devil's activities upon the earth. Do not be drawn into his clutches. Nothing on this earth is worth having or doing if it results in spending eternity with the devil in hell, in "the fire that never shall be quenched: Where their worm dieth not, and the fire is not quenched." (Mark 9:43-48)

THE BOTTOM LINE

We live in a time when great emphasis is placed on being tolerant. We should be considerate of others, but we can become so tolerant we have no standards.

The apostle Paul said the time will come when people will not listen to sound doctrine, but they shall heap unto themselves teachers who will tickle their itching ears with what they want to hear, thus turning the truth into a fable. (2 Timothy 4:3-4)

We see that today. People want to hear "smooth things" spoken from the pulpit, things that make them feel good so they can continue to live in their sins without reproach. (Proverbs 16:25, Isaiah 30:10)

Father God wanted to reconcile sinful man to Himself, so He sent His Dear Son our Lord Jesus Christ to earth in the likeness of men. God was in Christ reconciling the world unto Himself. (John 3:16-18, 2 Corinthians 5:19, Philippians 2:7)

Jesus knew no sin, but He was made sin for us that we might be made the righteousness of God in Him. (2 Corinthians 5:21)

There is no remission of sin without the shedding of blood, so Jesus willingly shed His Precious Innocent Blood to pay the penalty for our sin and rebellion against God. He bore the sin of the world in His Own Body and allowed Himself to be crucified on a cross. Jesus willingly sacrificed His flesh and died for our sins. He was buried and, hallelujah, He rose again the third day. He lives today and is our advocate (interceding for us) with Father God. (John 6:51, 10:15-18, Romans 8:11, 1 Corinthians 15:3-4, 13-14, Hebrews 9:12, 1 Peter 2:24, 1 John 2:1)

When we confess Jesus Christ as Savior, our past sins are remitted (erased) and Father covers us with a robe of the righteousness of Christ that we might be made the righteousness of God by faith in Christ. (Isaiah 61:10, Romans 5:1, 10:9-10, 2 Corinthians 5:21)

Because Christ sacrificed so much for you and for me, Father God honored Christ by requiring us to go through Christ to access Him. No one can go unto the Father except through Christ. All promises of God are fulfilled in Christ. (John 14:6, 2 Corinthians 1:20, Ephesians 2:18, 2 Timothy 1:1)

If we want our petitions answered, we must ask Father God in the Name of Jesus Christ. (John 16:23)

Some believe there are many paths to God, salvation and heaven. They are mistaken. Jesus is the way and the only way to God, salvation and heaven. (John 14:6, Acts 4:12, 1 John 5:10-15)

If we want to go to heaven when we leave here, we must confess Jesus Christ with our mouth and believe in our heart He is the Son of God, He died for our sins and God raised Him from the dead. (Romans 10:9-13, 1 Corinthians 15:3-8)

It matters not how good we are or what great philanthropic works we do, we will not spend eternity in heaven unless we confess Jesus Christ.

God highly exalted Jesus and gave Him a Name above every name. There is no other name under heaven given among men whereby we must be saved. (Acts 4:12, Romans 8:1-39, Philippians 2:9-11, Colossians 1:12-29)

So – the bottom line is: what have you done about Jesus?

As I said before, there are two kinds of people in the earth: those who belong to Jesus Christ and those who belong to satan.

Do you belong to Jesus Christ? or to satan?

DEAL WITH SELF FIRST

I've told this story before, but I believe the lesson learned is worth repeating.

My sister died on a Sunday evening. I was scheduled for jury duty the next morning.

On Monday morning, I went to the courthouse to get a postponement of my jury call. I got there early and sat on a bench in a large hall with other prospective jurors. After a little while, a woman got off the elevator and sat by me. Almost every word out of her mouth was a curse word – stretch your imagination.

I prayed quietly for God to help me deal with the situation. After a few minutes, the woman sat on the floor, put her head on the bench and went to sleep.

If I had said, "Lord, I'm in no mood to deal with this. Please do something about that woman," nothing would have been done.

I've learned when I ask God to help ME deal with a situation, He will take care of the other fellow.

Lesson learned: Whatever the situation, deal with self first.

EXCESSIVE

Thank God for preachers whose integrity is irreproachable. Sadly, it is questionable whether some preachers were called by God. (Matthew 24:11, 24, 2 Peter 2:1-3)

Occasionally, the news media raises questions about the integrity of some preacher when it comes to how he spends money people give to him for God's work. The preacher may try to defend himself or he may not. Either way, it seems to me the main point never is made.

Father God gives us the power to get wealth that he may establish His covenant with Abraham and He has plans for that money. God blessed Abraham to be a blessing and it is the same with us. We are merely stewards (managers) of all God has given to us. (Genesis 12:2, Deuteronomy 8:18)

It seems to me much of the preaching on prosperity is intended to justify the preacher's excessive lifestyle instead of teaching how to be good stewards of God's blessings.

Many people with fixed or limited income willingly and cheerfully deny themselves little niceties and sometimes things they need so they can give extra to God for the work He is doing through a particular preacher. When a preacher uses an excessive amount of the money he receives from sacrificial and other gifts to support an extravagant lifestyle, it can be considered as ill-gotten gain or even robbing God, so it is not surprising if the preacher eventually comes under scrutiny and censure.

God certainly intends for our needs to be met and He wants to give us the desires of our heart, but God definitely is against our being greedy. We need to be reasonable in what we want and make God's desires for us our desires. (Psalms 37:4-5, Proverbs 15:27, Philippians 4:15-19)

An airplane could be a need for a preacher who holds worldwide meetings and has a crew and equipment to take with him.

One ultra-luxury vehicle possibly might be justified, but a fleet of them would be excessive.

The same goes for homes. There is a difference in having a house which meets one's needs and having a mansion which rivals Buckingham Palace.

A preacher who tries to defend spending money meant for God's work on a lavish lifestyle often does so by telling people to look at his giving record instead of criticizing how much he lavishes on himself. That misses the point.

I have heard preachers say they give ten percent of all money that comes into their ministry to other ministries, outreaches, etc. It is important to tithe on our increase. That satisfies God's decree the tenth (tithe) is holy unto Him. Using this formula on an income of one million dollars, one hundred thousand dollars would go for God's work and nine hundred thousand would be left for ministry expenses and the preacher's personal use. (Leviticus 27:32, Deuteronomy 14:22, Proverbs 3:9-10, Malachi 3:8-11)

People should give to ministries which feed them spiritually, especially if they are fed on a regular basis, but some preachers ask people for sacrificial gifts. And some preachers even go so far as to tell people how much to give instead of letting God the Holy Spirit guide the givers in their giving. And then there are preachers who encourage people to include them as a beneficiary in their will. Preachers like these have a knack for making people feel guilty if they do not oblige them. (1 Corinthians 9:14)

People who give to a preacher to help accomplish God's work have a right to expect the preacher to use the money wisely and even sacrifice a little himself.

Many preachers brag how God has blessed them with material

blessings. Others try to hide their material blessings until some nosey reporter starts snooping around.

The point is, if such a preacher would cut back on his excessive lifestyle, he still could live very well and have more of God's money to use for God.

Now – say "Hallelujah" three times for all preachers whose integrity is irreproachable.

BETWEEN A ROCK AND A HARD PLACE

After Jesus was baptized by John the Baptist, the Holy Spirit led Jesus into the wilderness to be tempted by the devil. (Matthew 3:1--4:1, Luke 4:1-13)

I do not know if the Holy Spirit leads people into a wilderness today, but when God wants to train someone, He knows how to arrange the circumstances and we may think we are in a wilderness, or between a rock and a hard place, even if we are not.

One night in church some years ago, the Holy Spirit said very clearly to my spirit, "Will you die for me?" I believe I entered into an intensive training program by the Holy Spirit at that time. (Matthew 10:39, 1 Corinthians 15:31, Galatians 2:20, 5:24-25, 1 Peter 5:6)

Not long after, I said, "Lord, I could use a little vacation, just two or three days." The Holy Spirit said, "Do you want a vacation from God?" I said, "No! I want to take Him with me!"

Needless to say, I did not go on a vacation then and I still have not been on a vacation. I have been on a very few quick trips for business or spiritual renewal.

Another time, I was feeling pressed to finish something and I said, "Lord, it would be nice to go somewhere for two or three weeks where I would have nothing to do but work on this." I do not know how it happened, but I twisted my foot and ankle so badly I could not touch my foot to the floor for three weeks. That was not what I had in mind, but I had three weeks to do nothing except work on the project.

I believe God is trying to bring His Church up higher and conform us in a greater measure to the likeness of Jesus. (Romans 12:1-2)

God has something for every one of us to do for Him in these last days. To get us ready for His endtime work, God has to change some of us. Yet, when God tries to change us and we don't understand what He is doing, we fight Him, complain and do everything except cooperate with Him.

There may be things we are doing which are not wrong in themselves, yet they are not pleasing to God because He wants us to spend that time fellowshipping with Him or in a more productive way by doing something for Him.

When we wake up in the morning, it is a good idea to give the day to the Holy Spirit so we will be available to Him to work God's will during the day. We know all things can work together for our good. Things in good times and when we are between a rock and a hard place. If we stay attuned to the Holy Spirit, listen to Him and are quick to obey Him, by the end of the day, regardless of the circumstances, we will have peace and joy in our heart. And perhaps we will have grown a little more into the person God wants us to be and moved up a notch into His plan for us.

During these years of training, I have felt at times 1 Peter 4:12 was written just for me: "Beloved, think it not strange concerning the fiery trial which is to try you, as though some strange thing happened unto you." I'm sure some of you have felt the same at times.

My faith and trust in God have been tested and tried and both have grown stronger. I have learned to let the Holy Spirit have His way – right away. God always causes us to triumph in Christ. (1 Corinthians 15:57, 2 Corinthians 2:14)

There are things I want to do, but the Holy Spirit has said, "Wait," so I am waiting. They will come about in due time.

While we are waiting for the Lord to tell us to move on one thing, He will keep us busy doing something else for Him, so there is no idle time while waiting on the Lord. Even so, waiting on the Lord can try our patience at times because we want things to happen instantly, but there also is peace in flowing with the Lord to bring His will to pass.

I have heard numerous times we need to push for what we want. In other words, if God doesn't make something possible when we think He should, then go ahead with our plans and expect God to bless them. That does not seem wise, so I asked the Lord how we can know when to wait and when to push forward. He said to me through the Holy Spirit, "Wait until I tell you to move forward, then push." So until He tells me to move, I will wait on the Lord.

We live in the world, but we are not part of the world. Even so, if we are not extremely vigilant, we may slip somewhat into the world before we realize it. (Matthew 16:26, John 15:19, Romans 12:2)

After the devil had ended tempting Jesus, the devil departed from Jesus, but only "for a season." The devil always tries to come back after we have sent him packing. (Matthew 12:43-45, Luke 4:13)

The devil has used even family and friends to try to beguile me. Sometimes, I have taken a little bite before I have caught on. Other times, if I had not spoken up, I could have gotten off the narrow path God has me on which could have been a setback to my training.

One time, I was given a pretty necklace. It came with a poem which definitely was New Age. The necklace was from a very dear young person who did not know the meaning of the poem. The Holy Spirit convicted me to give back the necklace and explain why I could not wear it.

When I gave back the necklace, I was told by another person I could have thrown away the poem and kept the necklace. If I had done that, the young person would not have learned about the evils of the New Age. Besides, the necklace together with the poem represented the New Age, so it was wrong to keep it and most important, the Holy Spirit told me to give it back.

I hurt some feelings and I was sorry for it, but I had to take a deep breath and obey the Holy Spirit.

I promise you, the closer our walk with the Lord, the narrower our path becomes. (Matthew 7:13-14, Luke 12:48)

Some people will not stick with God's training when they get between a rock and a hard place, so they miss out on the vital work God has for them. (2 Timothy 2:3)

God was training someone I know for an important position and I was familiar with some of what he was going through. I can say he was between a rock and a hard place. After awhile, he decided he wanted out and moved on. Nothing he has tried to do for the Lord since has succeeded.

God can use any situation to train us: a difficult work environment, demanding and unappreciative family members, getting stuck in traffic with rude drivers, you name it. (Proverbs 3:11-12)

We cannot develop faith, patience and other godly traits unless we practice using them. Some of us need more practice than others. (Galatians 5:22-25, Ephesians 5:9)

If God put you where you are, and you know whether He did, please do not leave until He tells you to. That includes your church, your work, even where you live. He has a purpose for your being there.

God may be preparing you for something He has for you to do later, or you may be doing a work for Him where you are and you are not aware of it, or both. He can train us and use us for His good purposes at the same time.

I have spent a lot of time between a rock and a hard place, as some of you. Like some of you, I called it "surviving," but God actually was training me and using me in those situations. It could be years before I, or you, will use some of the training God has given us, but someday we will need it and we will be grateful for it. (Ecclesiastes 3:1)

Once we realize God is in control of all situations and He is trying to bring us up higher for His good purposes, it is easier to relax and go along with Him.

Many people speak of the cost of serving God. We may give up some things or God may take away some things. Things not pleasing to Him, things detrimental to our health and well-being or things which interfere with what He is trying to accomplish in us. He may even end some relationships. (Philippians 3:7, 13-14)

We may be grateful God took away some things and not so grateful He took away other things. And we may ask Him to take away things we want to give up.

At one time, I kept a cup of coffee on my desk at work almost all day. I asked God to take away my desire for coffee. He did. Since then, when someone opens a can of coffee, I say, "Ummm, that smells good," but I have absolutely no desire to drink any. Occasionally, I drink a cup of herbal (decaffeinated) tea.

Just as God through the Holy Spirit took away my desire for coffee, He can take away my desire to sin and make a way to escape when the devil tries to tempt me. (Mark 14:38, 1 Corinthians 10:13, 2 Timothy 4:18, 2 Peter 2:9)

When we surrender completely to God, we open the door to be of greater use to Him. After all, God has to make do with whomever He has and it might as well be you and me. (Psalms 37:3-6)

I do not want to miss out on anything God will allow me to do for Him in these last days. If that puts me between a rock and a hard place, Jesus will be there with me for He promised never to leave me nor forsake me. He will strengthen me and uphold me. He will not fail me. (Joshua 1:5, 1 Chronicles 28:9, Isaiah 1:19, 41:10, Daniel 11:32, John 14:12, Hebrews 13:5-6)

So – if you are being squeezed between a rock and a hard place and you don't know why, it may bc God is trying to get your attention.

Talk to Him about what He wants you to do for Him during these last days and then ask Him to remove any obstacles and give you the ability to do whatever it is. What He does may astound you. (1 Peter 4:11)

GOD IS A GOOD GOD

God is a good God. People say that all the time. Often they follow with the statement God has absolutely nothing to do with any "bad" thing which happens anywhere on the planet whether it is the result of nature on the rampage or anything else which adversely impacts our lives.

God does not tempt any person with evil. (Evil is birthed within the heart of man.) God does prove (test) us, try our hearts and chasten (discipline/train) us. (Job 1:8-12, 5:17-18, Psalms 66:10, Mark 7:20-23, James 1:3)

God does not chasten by giving us millions of dollars to spend on whatever we think will make us happy. Chastening is "grievous." (Hebrews 12:6-11)

Jesus said, "As many as I love, I rebuke and chasten: be zealous therefore, and repent." (Revelation 3:19)

Note Jesus said, "I" rebuke and chasten. The Lord is doing the rebuking and the chastening. It does not happen by chance. Here is further proof:

"My son, despise not thou the chastening of the Lord, nor faint when thou are rebuked of him. For whom the Lord loveth he chasteneth, and scourgeth every son whom he receiveth. If ye endure chastening, God dealeth with you as with sons; for what son is he whom the father chasteneth not?" Again, the Lord is doing the chastening. He chastens daughters as well as sons. (Galatians 3:28, Hebrews 12:5-11)

The Lord may use the Word (Scripture) to chasten us, He may remove the hedge He has around us as He did with Job or He may use some other means. Regardless of how it comes about, chastening is not pleasant, but it is for our good just as it was when our earthly parents chastened (disciplined) us. (Psalms 105:19, Proverbs 3:11-12, 2 Timothy 3:16)

Let's look at Job's test. Satan told God if He removed the hedge He had about Job and took away his substance, Job would curse God to His face. God told satan he could do anything to Job except kill him. Satan took away Job's children and his substance and put boils on him. Job stayed faithful to God. He did not sin or charge God foolishly. (Job 1:1-22, 2:1-6)

God was so pleased with Job for persevering with Him and making satan out to be the liar he is, God gave Job double what he had before. An added bonus: no women were as fair as the daughters of Job. (Job 42:10-17, John 8:44)

Note: God gave Job the same number of children because the first ten were alive in paradise (heaven). I wonder if the same wife gave birth to both sets of seven sons and three daughters. (Job 1:2, 42:10, 13)

It is important to note God gave satan permission to test Job. It also is important to note God limited satan in how far he could go in proving Job. (Job 2:6)

What about Sodom and Gomorrah? Was God a good God when He destroyed both cities and their inhabitants? (Genesis 19:24-25)

"The men of Sodom were wicked and sinners before the Lord exceedingly." Their iniquity was, in part, pride, idleness and neglect of the poor and needy while having "fullness of bread." They were haughty and committed abomination before the Lord. The Lord said, "I took them away as I saw good." In God's eyes, destroying Sodom and Gomorrah was a good thing because of their wickedness. (Genesis 13:13, 18:20--19:29, Ezekiel 16:49-50)

Was God a good God when He sentenced the children of Israel to wander forty years in the wilderness to humble them and to prove them, to know what was in their heart, whether they would keep His commandments that he might do them good at their latter end?

Note it was God who pronounced the sentence. (Numbers 14:25, 33, 23:19, 32:10-13, Deuteronomy 8:2, 16)

Now, suppose you had a child mired in sin and you turned your child over to God and asked God to save your child regardless of what it took. Soon after, your child was in a terrible accident and it took months for your child to heal. Would that be a good thing or a bad thing?

If it took something that drastic for God to get your child's attention and if your child gave his life to the Lord as a result of his experience, the final outcome would be a good thing because your child would be destined to spend eternity in heaven instead of in hell. Even so, many would insist the accident was a bad thing and God had nothing to do with it because all bad things come from satan. Yet, your child was saved as a result of your prayer. So, did God have a hand in bringing about, or allowing, the accident which brought about your child's salvation and the answer to your prayer?

Could your child have avoided the accident? Maybe. Maybe not. And maybe God sent an angel to prevent satan from killing your child, and then God used the accident to bring about good in your child's life. I do not know.

God does not want even one person to be lost to satan and He will take drastic measures to save someone, especially if there have been prayers for the person's salvation. He will honor His promise to deliver the seed of the righteous. To do that, it may be necessary "To deliver such an one unto satan for the destruction of the flesh that the spirit (the real person) may be saved in the day of the Lord Jesus." Could something similar have been involved in the above illustration? (1 Corinthians 5:5)

When we are chastened or something "bad" happens, it does not mean God is angry with us. It does not mean we have sinned.

When the disciples asked Jesus, "Master, who did sin, this man or his parents, that he was born blind?" Jesus answered, "Neither hath this man sinned, nor his parents: but that the works of God should be made manifest in him." (John 9:2-3, 1 Corinthians 10:11-12)

Our trials could be God is testing our faith and using us to bring about someone else's salvation at the same time. Or perhaps we have strayed somewhat from God and He is trying to bring us back to Him. Or perhaps God wants to remove some unworthy character trait from us and mature us until we are grounded and settled in our faith and in love so we can be more effective witnesses for Him, or for some other reason. (Ephesians 3:17-21, Colossians 1:21-24, 2 Timothy 1:9, 1 Peter 5:10)

We may be living for God and may not be aware of our need for the change God wants to make in us, but He knows our heart, so He knows us better than we know ourselves. (1 Samuel 16:7, James 4:8)

God knows what it will take to get us to the place He can work His perfect plan in us if we are willing. He even knows what it will take to make us willing. (Isaiah 1:19)

"The just shall live by faith" and our trials and temptations can put us in a fight to keep our faith.

Jesus was tempted "in all points" as we are, but He kept quoting the Word (Scripture) to satan and withstood satan's temptations. Jesus did not sin in the process and He has given us the ability to resist the devil and escape temptation. He will not allow us to be tempted above what we are able to bear. (Matthew 4:1-11, 1 Corinthians 10:13, Ephesians 6:10-18, Hebrews 4:15, James 1:12-16, 4:7, 2 Timothy 4:18)

God knows how strong our faith is and how we will react to adversity. In truth, we may react completely opposite of how we think we will.

The apostle Peter was certain he never would deny Jesus, but he did – three times. (Matthew 26:31-75, Mark 16:7)

It is important WE know our faith will not fail us and we will not give up or turn away from God in the midst of what He calls us to do regardless of how difficult the tasking. We must be dependable if God is to use us. The apostle Peter ended his life a devoted follower of Christ.

The trial of our faith is much more precious than gold. Our trials can inspire us to exercise our faith. Trials can strengthen our faith and prepare us for work the Lord has for us to do at the appropriate time. (1 Peter 1:7)

Some of the "bad" things we experience may be our reaping what we have sown. Or maybe they are manifestations of idle words we have spoken. Or maybe we were "beguiled" by satan and gave in to the temptations satan brought before us. Or maybe we were attacked by satan. (Genesis 3:13, Matthew 12:36-37, Mark 11:23, Galatians 6:7-8, 1 Peter 5:8)

What about hurricanes, earthquakes, tornadoes, floods and other so-called acts of nature? Are they natural phenomena, and God has nothing to do with them, or are they a result of God's judgment coming upon the earth? There seems to be a lot of controversy over the reason(s) for the great devastation now shaking the earth.

Isaiah 45:7 says, "I form the light, and create darkness: I make peace, and create evil: I the Lord do all these things." I compared several Bibles and found where substitutions were made in this verse for "evil," the most used were "calamity" and "disaster." Strong's Concordance also includes these words for "evil" in this verse. ("Evil" used here does not mean "sin" because, again, sin originates in the heart.) (Jeremiah 28:15-17, Mark 7:20-23)

God may create calamities and disasters to get people's attention so they will turn to Him, repent and be saved. One example is when God sent an earthquake to break Paul and Silas out of prison and save the jailer and others. (Acts 16:19-40)

A lady who calls herself a Scribe for God said the Holy Spirit told her, "Man has his puny weapons, but God has nature. Who can withstand the forces of nature?" Look around at the devastation nature is causing in the earth today. God is trying to get people saved before it is too late. (For a partial list of endtime events, read these chapters: Matthew 24, Mark 13.)

Regardless, "the sufferings of this present time are not worthy to be compared with the glory which shall be revealed in us." (Romans 8:17-18, 2 Timothy 2:11-13, 1 Peter 2:21-25)

Christ suffered for us and if we followers of Christ (Christians) suffer for Him, we are "partakers of Christ's sufferings" and shall live with Him and reign with Him, so let us "glorify God on this behalf." (Hebrews 3:14, 2 Timothy 2:12, 1 Peter 4:13, 16-19, 5:1)

If our test or trial is an attack on our body, we need to exercise our authority in the Name of Jesus Christ and claim and receive our healing. Our healing may manifest at once or we may have to walk through the problem for awhile, but if we do not abandon our fight of faith in the Name of Jesus Christ our Savior, Lord, Master and Healer, and in God's Word which says we are healed, we will overcome. (Matthew 8:7, 17, 23:8-12, Mark 11: 22-26, John 13:13, 1 Peter 2:24, Revelation 12:11)

God takes no pleasure in those who draw back (backslide). Knowing this can drive us to persevere in our faith and believe God and His Word over an extended period of time even though everything seems to be going against us and, thus, drive us on to victory. (Mark 4:17-19, Hebrews 10:38)

"The just shall live by faith." Jesus made it clear. He said, "Be not afraid, only believe" – "Have faith in God" – "According to your faith be it unto you" – "…as thou hast believed, so be it done unto thee" – "…thy faith hath made thee whole." (Matthew 8:13, 9:22, 29, Mark 5:34, 36, 11:22, Romans 1:17, Galatians 3:11)

God will do for us only what we believe in our heart He will do, so it is by our faith we will stand and overcome our troubles and afflictions.

We cannot hide from God and nothing can happen to us without His knowledge and permission. And, yes, God does allow unpleasant things to happen to us for our benefit even though we may not see any benefit at the time – "troubles are a part of God's plan for us Christians." (1 Thessalonians 3:3 TLB, 1 Peter 5:10)

Whatever happens to us, we can be certain Lord Jesus Christ will go through our hard times with us and God will give us victory through the Lord if we will believe Him and trust in Him with our whole heart - greater is the Holy Spirit in us than satan in the world. (Psalms 28:7, 33:21, 34:8, 9l:15, Isaiah 54:17, 1 Corinthians 15:57, Hebrews 13:5, 2 Timothy 4:17-18, 1 John 4:4)

Chastening can inspire us to conform to the image of Jesus in greater measure, develop deeper intimacy with Jesus and greater sensitivity to the Holy Spirit and, thus, a closer walk with God. It can work patience in us and build endurance as we endure the chastening. Chastening is meant to bring forth good in our lives. Yes, "all things work together for good to them that love God, to them who are the called according to his purpose." And God has a purpose and a plan for each of us. (Genesis 50:20, Jeremiah 29:11, Romans 5:3-4, 8:28, 1 Corinthians 2:9, 2 Timothy 1:9, 1 John 4:4, 5:4-5)

God sent Jesus Christ and "God was in Christ, reconciling the world unto himself." Jesus gave His life (flesh) as a sacrifice for the life of the world. Jesus endured the cross, despising the shame of it, to save lost souls and give us saved eternal life and life on earth more abundantly. Yes, Jesus and all He accomplished on the cross are paramount, but we should not ignore the many Scriptures which say the Lord is a God of Judgment because He is. One day each of us, saved and unsaved, will stand before The Judgment Seat of Christ, but we can count on Him to judge the world with righteousness and the people with equity. (Psalms 98:9, John 3:15-17, 10:15-18, Romans 14:10, 1 Corinthians 15:14, 2 Corinthians 5:19, Hebrews 12:2, 1 Peter 4:17-18, Revelation 20:13)

God's ways are higher than our ways and His thoughts are higher than our thoughts. Even so, we can be assured God loves us unconditionally and nothing can separate us from His love which is in Jesus Christ our Lord. (Isaiah 55:8-9, John 3:16, Romans 8:35-39)

The Lord allowed a messenger of satan to buffet the apostle Paul to keep him humble. Paul asked the Lord three times to remove that "thorn," but the Lord did not. Paul changed his attitude and said, "Most gladly therefore will I rather glory in my infirmities, that the power of Christ may rest upon me. Therefore I take pleasure in infirmities, in reproaches, in necessities, in persecutions, in distresses for Christ's sake: for when I am weak then am I strong." (Could some of us need a change of attitude?) (2 Corinthians 11:23-31, 12:7-10)

God created us for His pleasure and we cannot please Him without faith, so think how pleased God is when we His children persevere in our faith in spite of our challenges. (Hebrews 11:6, Revelation 4:11)

The hard things we go through may be the very things which will propel us into God's perfect plan and bless us beyond our wildest dreams.

Some people say God is not in control – we are. True, God gave us dominion over the earth, but Adam gave it to satan, so satan is the god of this world and he spends all of his time trying to deceive us and devour us, but God has ultimate control. (Genesis 1:26, Psalms 115:16, 2 Corinthians 4:4, 1 Peter 5:8)

Consider the miracles in your life, great things you cannot explain and your innumerable prayers God has answered. The Old Testament book of Daniel says God removes kings, sets up kings and gives kingdoms to whomsoever He will. God has not changed. There are no "coincidences" in life. (Psalms 103:19, Jeremiah 18:7-10, 27:5, Daniel 2:21, 4:3, 17, 35)

We who are saved – who have confessed Jesus is the Son of God, He died for our sins and God raised Him from the dead – have the

Holy Spirit dwelling in us to help us, strengthen us, comfort us, guide us and give us the ability to do whatever God wants us to do. We need to welcome the Holy Spirit and give Him our fullest cooperation. (Psalms 27:11, 30:10, 32:8, 37:23, Proverbs 3:6, Matthew 23:8-12, John 14:16, Romans 8:26-27, 10:9-10, 1 Corinthians 15:3-4, Hebrews 13:20-21, 1 Peter 4:11, 1 John 5:6-8)

Jesus came to destroy the works of the devil. He redeemed us from the curse of the law. He bore our sins in His own body on the cross that we should live unto righteousness. He also took our infirmities and bore our sicknesses on the cross and by His stripes we are healed. He will deliver us out of our afflictions and troubles if we trust in Him and believe He will. If you have not already done so, make Jesus Christ your Savior, Lord and Master now and let the love God will shed abroad in your heart by the Holy Spirit dominate you. (Psalms 30:2, 31:1, 14, 34:15-22, Isaiah 53:5, Matthew 8:17, Mark 11:22-26, Romans 5:5, 2 Corinthians 5:21, Galatians 3:13, 2 Timothy 4:18, 1 Peter 2:24, 1 John 3:8)

God keeps a watchful eye over all of His creation and whoever is born of God (saved) overcomes the world. (Psalms 34:15-19, Luke 12:6-7, 22-30, 1 John 4:4, 12, 16, 5:3-4)

"The earth is the Lord's and the fullness thereof; the world, and they that dwell therein." The Lord's Word and His Holy Spirit will direct our steps as we will allow, but the Holy Spirit will not take away our freedom to make our own choices. (Psalms 24:1, 37:23)

Never forget God is a good God and He wants only good for us - "no good thing will he withhold from them that walk uprightly" - but what may be good for one person may cause another person to stumble and sin. Also, we may have to go through some "bad stuff" to get to God's best for us, so it is important to cooperate with Him, trust in Him and keep our faith in Him strong during the hard times as well as the good times. We do this by keeping God's Word ever before us, believing it in our heart and doing His Word instead of allowing negative thoughts, feelings and words to escape our lips. Again – remember, we walk by faith and not by sight, and it is by faith we stand until victory comes. Since faith comes by the Word of God, read the Word every day and take into your heart what you read. And pay close attention to the leading of the Holy Spirit and obey Him. (Proverbs 16:3; Isaiah 42:8, Romans 10:17, 2 Corinthians 1:24, 5:7, Philippians 4:8, James 1:22)

"So if you are suffering according to God's will, keep on doing what is right and trust yourself to the God who made you, for he will never fail you." His truth and his mercy are everlasting. And be sure to give God all the glory. (Psalms 100:5, 106:1, James 5:10-12, 1 Peter 4:19 (TLB))

Jesus said He rebukes and chastens those He loves, so we can say the Lord rebukes us and chastens us for our own good because He loves us. (Hebrews 12:6, Revelation 3:19)

"Oh that men would praise the Lord for his goodness, and for his wonderful works to the children of men!" (Psalms 107:8,15,31, James 1:17)

Say with the psalmist: "God is the Lord, which hath shown us light…Thou art my God, and I will praise thee: thou art my God, I will exalt thee." (Psalms 118:27-29)

Yes, God is a good God.

A very good God.

SOME POWERFUL SCRIPTURES

These powerful Scriptures can help in many situations.

Be sure to ask God in the Name of Jesus except where Jesus gave us authority to command something in His Name. (See chapter, "The Catalyst.")

Speak the Scriptures out loud.

Psalm 25:2: O my God, I trust in thee: let me not be ashamed, let not mine enemies triumph over me.

Psalm 34:4: I sought the Lord and he heard me, and delivered me from all my fears.

Psalm 30:10: Hear, O Lord, and have mercy upon me: Lord, be thou my helper.

Psalm 118:17: I shall not die, but live, and declare the works of the Lord.

John 16:23, Jesus speaking: …Verily, verily, I say unto you, Whatsoever ye shall ask the Father in my name, he will give it you.

Matthew 21:22, Jesus speaking: And all things, whatsoever ye shall ask in prayer, believing, ye shall receive.

Mark 11:22-26, Jesus speaking:
22 Have faith in God.
23 For verily I say unto you, That whosoever shall say unto this mountain, Be thou removed, and be thou cast into the sea; and shall

not doubt in his heart, but shall believe that those things which he saith shall come to pass; he shall have whatsoever he saith.

24 Therefore I say unto you, What things soever ye desire, when ye pray, believe that ye receive them, and ye shall have them.

25 And when ye stand praying, forgive, if ye have aught against any: that your Father also which is in heaven may forgive you your trespasses.

26 But if ye do not forgive, neither will your Father which is in heaven forgive your trespasses.

2 Timothy 4:18: And the Lord shall deliver me from every evil work, and will preserve me unto his heavenly kingdom: to whom be glory for ever and ever. Amen.

Jeremiah 30:17: For I will restore health unto thee, and I will heal thee of thy wounds, saith the Lord....

Psalm 30:2: O Lord my God, I cried unto thee, and thou hast healed me.

Matthew 8:17: ...Himself (Jesus) took our infirmities, and bare our sicknesses.

1 Peter 2:24: Who his own self bare our sins in his own body on the tree, that we, being dead to sins, should live unto righteousness: by whose stripes ye were healed. (I've been healed by the stripes of Jesus.)

Acts 9:34: ...Jesus Christ maketh thee (has made me) whole....

Psalm 34:19: Many are the afflictions of the righteous: but the Lord delivereth him out of them all.

Isaiah 54:17: No weapon that is formed against thee shall prosper; and every tongue that shall rise against thee in judgment thou shalt condemn. This is the heritage of the servants of the Lord, and their righteousness is of me, saith the Lord.

Psalm 34:22: The Lord redeemeth the soul of his servants: and none of them that trust in him shall be desolate.

Psalm 27:14: Wait on the Lord: be of good courage, and he shall strengthen thine heart: wait, I say, on the Lord. (Psalm 31:24)

Psalm 28:7: The Lord is my strength and my shield; my heart trusted in him, and I am helped: therefore my heart greatly rejoiceth; and with my song will I praise him.

Psalm 29:11: The Lord will give strength unto his people; the Lord will bless his people with peace.

1 John 4:4: Ye are of God, little children, and have overcome them: because greater is he (the Holy Spirit) that is in you, than he (satan) that is in the world.

Revelation 12:11: And they overcame him (satan) by the blood of the Lamb, and by the word of their testimony; and they loved not their lives unto the death.

Deuteronomy 33:25: …as thy days, so shall thy strength be.

2 Timothy 1:7: For God hath not given us the spirit of fear; but of power, and of love, and of a sound mind.

1 Corinthians 2:16: …we (I) have the mind of Christ.

James 5:16: …pray one for another, that ye may be healed. The effectual fervent prayer of a righteous man availeth much.

Isaiah 41:10: Fear thou not; for I am with thee: be not dismayed; for I am thy God: I will strengthen thee; yea, I will help thee; yea, I will uphold thee with the right hand of my righteousness.

Joshua 1:5: …I will be with thee: I will not fail thee, nor forsake thee.

Psalm 34:8: O taste and see that the Lord is good: blessed is the man that trusteth in him.

SALVATION PRAYER

What must I do to be saved? (Acts16:30)

Believe on the Lord Jesus Christ, and you shall be saved. (Acts 16:31)

If you confess with your mouth the Lord Jesus Christ and believe in your heart Christ died for our sins and God raised Him from the dead, you shall be saved, for with the heart man believes unto righteousness and with his mouth confession is made unto salvation. (Romans 5:8, 10:9-10)

Whosoever shall call upon the Name of the Lord shall be saved. (Romans 10:13)

Jesus said, "…him that cometh to me I will in no wise cast out" (not turn away). (John 6:37)

CONFESSION:

Father God,

I come to you in the Name of Jesus Christ.

I am a sinner. (Luke 13:3, Acts 2:38, Romans 3:23-26)

I repent of my sins and ask You to forgive me.

I believe in my heart:

Jesus Christ is Your Son. (John 6:69)

He died to pay the penalty for my sins and you raised Him from the dead the third day. (Romans 4:25, 5:8, 1 Corinthians 15:3-4)

Jesus Christ said if I come to Him, He will accept me, so I call upon His Name. (John 6:37)

I believe in my heart:

I have been forgiven. (Romans 3:25, 1 John 1:9-10)

My entire past has been erased.

I am a new creature in Jesus Christ. (2 Corinthians 5:17)

I am saved. (2 Corinthians 5:21, 1 John 1:9)

I make Jesus Christ my Lord. (John 13:13, Philippians 2:11)

Help me to live for You and fulfill Your plan for me. (Jeremiah 29:11, 1 Corinthians 3:9, 2 Corinthians 5:20, 2 Timothy 1:9)

Thank You, Father God.

In the Name of Jesus Christ.

If you prayed this prayer, I strongly suggest you ask Lord Jesus Christ to direct you to a Bible-based church where the true Word of God is preached in love. (Ephesians 1:3, 1:13, 4:15, Colossians 1:5-6)

God bless you.

OTHER BOOKS
BY BILLIE JOE

A GUIDE FOR LIVING IN THESE PERILOUS TIMES
ISBN 1-4033-2223-6 (sc-Paperback)
ISBN 1-4033-2222-8 (e-book)

We are living in perilous times with wars, plagues, terrorists and evil all around us. Jesus said He will give divine protection to us who stay close by His side. This book can serve as a guide for living victoriously during these perilous times. Prepare for the soon coming of our Lord Jesus Christ.

CONFESSIONS OF A BELIEVER
ISBN 978-1-4259-9102-9 (sc-Paperback)
ISBN 978-1-4343-0802-3 (e-book)

We get what we say (confess). That includes our idle, or casual, words, good and bad. The Bible makes that very clear.

The things we confess may not come to pass immediately, but I am sure many of us can think of more than one adult whose life followed what was spoken over him as a child or he spoke over himself and his life ended tragically.

This book can help us get into the habit of confessing blessings, instead of curses, into our lives and over our loved ones, while guiding and enhancing our praise and worship time with our Lord Jesus Christ.

FODDER TO CHEW ON, Book One

ISBN 978-1-4343-5085-5 (sc-Paperback)
ISBN 978-1-4343-5088-6 (e-book)

This book includes over twenty topics of interest to almost everyone. Some are:
– The human spirit and cloning of humans.
– A comparison of The Virtuous Woman of the Bible with today's woman.
– Facts on The Battle of Armageddon.
– How to have peace in our heart.
– Revealing comments on the male species.

You are sure to appreciate the gentle humor and insight into human nature.

These books may be ordered from:
The publisher: 1-888-280-7715
Online book sellers
Your local bookstore

These books can help clear up questions you may have about the Bible. They can help you develop a more personal relationship with the Lord. Our souls are too precious and our choice of an eternal home is too final for us to be guided by misinformation. These books are based on the Bible as the liberal Scriptures provided confirm.

These books are for all–Christians and non-Christians.

ABOUT THE AUTHOR

Billie Joe was saved at a young age.

After the premature death of her husband, she began to seek God for new direction and a closer relationship with Him.

Sometimes, she would read a verse of Scripture and say, "Lord, I believe that, but I don't know what to do with it." The Holy Spirit always led her to the answer, but sometimes in unusual ways.

Later, when she became dissatisfied with her denomination, the Holy Spirit led her to a Spirit-filled, Bible-based church where she served in various ministries.

Billie Joe writes under the guidance of the Holy Spirit and provides supporting Scriptures for the reader's review.

Billie Joe resides in Texas.